*The glory of the country is my
own glory—to raise the Russian Empire
to a degree of power above that of the
other empires of Asia and Europe.*

Catherine the Great

For Anthony and Alyssa, who love a wicked good story.

Photographs © 2009: akg-Images, London: 47 (Vigilius Erichsen), 74 top (Vassily Grigorievich Perov), 105 (Library of Congress), 72 top, 74 center, 99 (RIA Nowosti), 56, 73 center left (State History Museum, Moscow/RIA Nowosti), 17, 29, 72 bottom, 73 bottom, 75 top, 80, 89, 113; Art Resource, NY: 84 (Vigilius Erichsen/Erich Lessing), 51 (New York Public Library), 62 (Ruth Schacht/Bildarchiv Preussischer Kulturbesitz); Bridgeman Art Library International Ltd., London/New York: 95 (Archives du Ministere des Affaires Estrangeres, Paris, France/Archives Charmet), 30, 70 bottom (Art Gallery of Taganrog), 67 (C.L. Doughty/Private Collection/©Look and Learn), 60 (Nikolai Nikolajevitch Gay/Tretyakov Gallery, Moscow, Russia), 33 (Georg Christoph Grooth/Odessa Fine Arts Museum, Ukraine), 37, 70 center (Georg Christoph Grooth/Tretyakov Gallery, Moscow, Russia); Corbis Images: 73 top (Bettmann), 25, 70 top (Georg Christoph Grooth/©Reproduced by permission of the State Hermitage Museum, St. Petersburg, Russia), 10 (Fyodor Rokotov/Alfredo Dagli Orti/The Art Archive), 73 center right, 82 (Roland Weihrauch/dpa), 75 bottom, 117 (Richard Woodman/Bettmann), 121 (Adam Woolfitt); Getty Images/Hulton Archive: 42, 49; Mary Evans Picture Library: 71 center, 71 top, 100; North Wind Picture Archives: 22; The Art Archive/Picture Desk: 21 (Georg Christoph Grooth/Musée du Château de Versailles/Gianni Dagli Orti), 41 (Odorando Montule/Biblioteca Nazionale Marciana Venice/Alfredo Dagli Orti); The Granger Collection, New York: 72 center (Stefano Torelli), 74 bottom, 109 (Richard Caton Woodville); 45, 86, 93; The Image Works: 68, 71 bottom (Roger-Viollet), 79 (The Print Collector/Heritage).

Illustrations by XNR Productions, Inc.: 4, 5, 8, 9
Cover art, page 8 inset by Mark Summers
Chapter art by Raphael Montoliu

Library of Congress Cataloging-in-Publication Data

Vincent, Zu, 1952-
Catherine the Great : empress of Russia / Zu Vincent.
p. cm. — (A wicked history)
Includes bibliographical references and index.
ISBN-13: 978-0-531-21802-0 (lib. bdg.) 978-0-531-20738-3 (pbk.)
ISBN-10: 0-531-21802-3 (lib. bdg.) 0-531-20738-2 (pbk.)
1. Catherine II, Empress of Russia, 1729-1796—Juvenile literature. 2.
Empresses—Russia—Biography—Juvenile literature. 3.
Russia—History—Catherine II, 1762-1796—Juvenile literature. I.
Title.
DK170.V54 2009
947'.063092—dc22
[B]

2008041543

No part of this publication may be reproduced in whole or in part, or stored in a retrieval system, or transmitted in any form or by any means, electronic, mechanical, photocopying, recording, or otherwise, without written permission of the publisher. For information regarding permission, write to Scholastic Inc., 557 Broadway, New York, NY 10012.

Tod Olson, Series Editor
Marie O'Neill, Art Director
Allicette Torres, Cover Design
SimonSays Design!, Book Design and Production

© 2009 Scholastic Inc.

All rights reserved. Published by Franklin Watts, an imprint of Scholastic Inc. Published simultaneously in Canada. Printed in the United States of America.

SCHOLASTIC, FRANKLIN WATTS, and associated logos are trademarks and/or registered trademarks of Scholastic Inc.

1 2 3 4 5 6 7 8 9 10 R 18 17 16 15 14 13 12 11 10 09   23

Catherine the Great

Empress of Russia

ZU VINCENT

Franklin Watts®
An Imprint of Scholastic Inc.
New York Toronto London Auckland Sydney
Mexico City New Delhi Hong Kong
Danbury, Connecticut

The World of Catherine the Great

During her 34-year reign, Catherine expanded the borders of Russia and earned the respect of the rest of Europe.

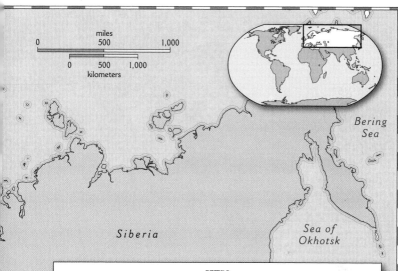

miles
0   500   1,000

0   500   1,000
kilometers

Bering Sea

Siberia

Sea of Okhotsk

KEY

Ⓐ Princess Sophie (later called Catherine the Great) was born in Stettin in 1729.

Ⓑ Sophie arrived in the Russian capital in 1745, hoping to marry Peter, heir to the Russian throne.

Ⓒ In 1762, Catherine seized the throne of Russia from her husband, Tsar Peter III. Peter was murdered a few weeks later.

Ⓓ In 1774, Russia obtained access to Black Sea ports after a war with the Ottoman Turks.

Ⓔ Catherine's troops crushed Pugachev's peasant revolt in 1774.

Ⓕ Catherine annexed the Crimea in 1783.

Ⓖ Catherine the Great died in 1796.

Lands Catherine Acquired
▧ Territory taken from the Ottoman Empire
▦ Territory taken from Poland

Map is a Lambert Azimuthal equal-area projection, not a Mercator projection.

TABLE OF CONTENTS

A Wicked Web

Catherine's Family

**PRINCE CHRISTIAN AUGUST
OF ANHALT-ZERBST**
Catherine's father; general in
the Prussian army

**PRINCESS JOHANNA OF
ANHALT-ZERBST**
Catherine's mother

ELIZABETH I
Catherine's mother-in-law;
empress of Russia from
1741 to 1762

PETER III
Catherine's husband; nephew and
adopted son of Elizabeth I; tsar of
Russia for six months in 1762

PAUL I
Catherine's eldest son; ruled
Russia from 1796 to 1801

**CATHERINE
THE GREAT**

ANNA PETROVNA
Catherine's daughter

ALEXIS GRIGORYEVICH
Catherine's son by
Gregory Orlov

Friends and Lovers

❧❧❧❧❧❧❧❧❧❧❧❧❧❧❧❧❧❧❧❧❧❧❧❧

SERGEI SALTYKOV
Russian officer;
possible father of
Catherine's son Paul

CHARLES HANBURY-WILLIAMS
British envoy to Russia and friend
of Catherine

STANISLAS PONIATOWSKI
possible father of
Catherine's daughter, Anna;
later king of Poland

GREGORY ORLOV
Russian officer and father of
Catherine's son Alexis

ALEXIS ORLOV
Gregory's brother and commander
of the Russian navy

GREGORY POTEMKIN
Russian officer and the love
of Catherine's life

ALEXEI BESTUZHEV
Russian chancellor; in charge
of foreign policy under Elizabeth I

Opponents and Enemies

❧❧❧❧❧❧❧❧❧❧❧❧❧❧❧❧❧❧❧❧❧❧❧❧

IVAN VI
infant emperor of Russia from 1740
to 1741; overthrown by Elizabeth

FREDERICK II
king of Prussia from
1740 to 1786

MUSTAFA III
sultan of the Ottoman Empire
from 1757 to 1774

ABDÜLHAMID I
brother of Mustafa;
sultan of the Ottoman Empire
from 1774 to 1789

EMILIAN PUGACHEV
leader of Russian peasant
revolt; executed by Catherine

ALEXANDER RADISHCHEV
writer exiled to
Siberia by Catherine

CATHERINE THE GREAT, 1729–1796

CATHERINE EMERGED FROM THE TSAR'S palace and gazed down the massive stairs to the courtyard below. Thousands of soldiers stood in formation, waiting for the future of Russia to unfold. The 32-year-old wife of Tsar Peter III strode down the palace steps, long hair flying, dressed in the uniform of a Russian soldier. Her message was clear: Peter no longer commanded the army or the state. Catherine was seizing the throne of Russia from her husband.

At the base of the steps, Catherine jumped on a white horse and set off through the streets of St. Petersburg. Nearly 14,000 loyal soldiers followed close behind. Peter still led a small force of bodyguards, holed up just a few miles away. The new empress of Russia rode hard, her army at her heels. She surprised the tsar's bodyguards and convinced them to surrender without a fight.

While Peter awaited his fate, Catherine wrote out a formal document for him to sign and gave it to a messenger. The tsar wept as he read the paper. "Take me to the empress," he begged.

Catherine refused to see her husband. She had him stripped of his uniform and his sword. Peter was humiliated. The woman he had been married to for ten years had utterly betrayed him. He signed the paper and collapsed like a rag doll.

Meanwhile, Catherine sat down to dine with her soldiers. She celebrated with just half a glass of wine. She knew, after all, that her coup was not yet complete. As long as Peter lived, he could rally support and take back the throne.

A few short weeks later, Catherine received a secret note from one of her most loyal aides. "Little Mother, he is no more!" the note read. Peter III of Russia—her husband since she was 16 years old—had been murdered.

Catherine tucked the note deep into her drawer

and turned the key. People would suspect that she had ordered the killing, but without the letter there would be no proof.

Catherine had been edging closer and closer to this moment since 1744, when she arrived in Russia to marry a duke she barely knew and did not like. To win acceptance in her new country, she learned to speak the language and converted to the Russian Orthodox faith. She made powerful friends. Now those friends had helped her pull off one of the most stunning coups in history.

It had taken 18 years for a minor German princess to transform herself into the ruler of Russia. She would spend the next three decades making her reputation as Catherine the Great.

PART 1

Princess Sophie

Friederike

Auguste

Groomed for a Royal Marriage

A strong-willed tomboy
LEARNS TO BE A PRINCESS.

THE FUTURE RULER OF THE VAST RUSSIAN Empire began her life as princess of a tiny German-speaking state that could have dropped off the map of Europe without much notice. She was born on May 2, 1729, as Sophie Friederike Auguste of Anhalt-Zerbst.

Anhalt-Zerbst lay in the center of present-day Germany, a region covered in forest, pasture, and bog. It had recently become part of the expanding Prussian

Empire. Sophie's father, Prince Christian August, served as a general in the powerful Prussian army, which was fast becoming the envy and terror of the major powers of Europe. He governed the grim city of Stettin, a military outpost on the eastern edge of the empire.

But Prince Christian's titles gave little comfort to Sophie's mother, who found Stettin unbearably dull. Johanna was a princess herself and came from a much more powerful family than her husband's. But her parents had fallen on hard times and were forced to marry her off when she was 15. Johanna felt she

SOPHIE GREW UP in Stettin, a seaport on the Prussian border that her father governed. Her mother hoped to escape Stettin by marrying Sophie into a royal family.

deserved a better life—and her daughter was going to help her get it.

As soon as Sophie learned to walk, Princess Johanna began grooming her for a marriage into one of Europe's important royal families. Servants and ladies-in-waiting hovered over Sophie. Tutors schooled her in the German Lutheran faith. They taught her dance, music, and language.

Bright and chatty, Sophie took to her lessons well. Before she turned five she could read French, the language of Europe's most sophisticated elite. Princess Johanna, who loved to travel, brought her little girl to royal parties in nearby states. Sophie quickly learned to feel at home among Europe's princes and princesses.

Despite her mother's attempts to mold her for marriage, Sophie developed a mind of her own. She grew restless in the parlors of the rich and liked to mingle with the common children of Stettin. As soon as she was old enough, she developed a passion for horseback riding and bird hunting.

Sophie's independence made her mother furious. Princess Johanna was certain that such a willful girl would never be welcomed into the finest royal families.

When Sophie was seven, her chances for a good marriage suffered a major blow. A respiratory illness kept her confined to her bed for nearly a month. When she recovered, violent coughing fits had left her spine twisted. Her right shoulder sat higher than the left, and her back looked deformed.

Princess Johanna was horrified. If Sophie remained disfigured she would never make a good match. Johanna secretly summoned the local bonesetter—who also happened to be Stettin's executioner.

The bonesetter made a stiff corset to straighten Sophie's back. Princess Johanna made sure that her daughter wore it day and night. It hurt terribly and ruined Sophie's appetite. But she consoled herself with books, spending countless hours hidden in her parents' library. After many months, her back finally straightened. By then, Sophie had been reduced to skin and bone. Only gradually did she regain her strength.

Despite her daughter's infirmities, Princess Johanna vowed to find Sophie a desirable marriage. Whenever she could get an invitation, she dragged her daughter 70 miles southwest to Berlin to present her at the court of the Prussian king, Frederick II.

In 1740, Johanna's efforts began to pay off. Frederick II had big plans in Europe and thought the spirited young princess from Anhalt-Zerbst could be of some use. He decided to recommend her as a match for a German-speaking duke named Peter Ulrich. Peter was related to both the Swedish and Russian royal families. That made the 12-year-old duke one of the most eligible bachelors on earth.

Just 11 years old, Sophie had become a pawn in a vast struggle for power in Europe. King Frederick II was gearing up for war with his archenemy, Austria. He wanted his neighbor to the east, Russia, on his side. A Prussian wife for Peter could be just what was needed to help the alliance along.

Sophie had a dim understanding of her role in the king's plans when she met Peter at a royal party later that year. He looked skinny and sickly, and he wouldn't talk about anything except soldiers. But Sophie noticed that mothers with marriageable daughters followed him everywhere he went. She decided that Peter might be as dull as a rock. But that didn't matter. One day, he could be in a position of great power. For now, that was all she needed to know.

PETER WAS ONE OF the world's most eligible bachelors. He was also immature and probably not very bright.

AN UNDERDEVELOPED EMPIRE

RUSSIA IN THE 1740s WAS A VAST EMPIRE, sharply divided between rich and poor. It stretched 5,500 miles from Poland in the west to the Pacific Ocean in the east. Of its 19 million people, only 50,000 were landowners. Most of the population lived as serfs—peasants who were legally bound to work for their landlords.

Most Western Europeans thought Russia was stuck in the past. Its vast, snowy plains were largely undeveloped. Russians had little access to education—and just one university. They suffered under tyrannical rulers. In Western Europe, kings and queens were beginning to give up power to parliaments and legislatures. In Russia, the tsars could still make laws and imprison enemies without consulting anyone.

SERFS USING crude tools to farm their master's fields. Russia trailed the rest of Europe in education, technology, and wealth.

CHAPTER 2

"The Most Brilliant"

Sophie wins a chance to
marry an heir and SETS OFF
FOR HER NEW HOME.

IN NOVEMBER 1741, THE YEAR AFTER SOPHIE
met Peter, the young duke became even more desirable
as a husband. His aunt in Russia, Elizabeth Petrovna,
shocked the world by seizing the Russian throne from
her distant cousin, the infant ruler Ivan VI. She locked
Ivan and his mother away and ordered their guards

23

to shoot them if they tried to escape. Elizabeth then declared herself empress of all Russia.

Most important to Sophie was what happened next. The childless empress adopted her nephew, Peter. She brought him to Russia, where he gave up his right to become Sweden's king. Now the young duke was free to inherit the Russian throne.

But would Elizabeth consider Sophie a good match for the next tsar of Russia? Princess Johanna did her best to ensure that the empress would. She took Sophie to Berlin to sit for a portrait. The small painting made the most of Sophie's looks. It was sent off to the Russian capital of St. Petersburg for the court to consider.

Weeks passed, and Sophie grew nervous. She knew that other young women had sent their portraits to St. Petersburg, hoping for Peter's hand. Surely those women weren't burdened with Sophie's long nose and pointed chin.

Still, Sophie felt she had an advantage. She was no empty-headed beauty. She had read widely on all the important topics of the day. She displayed character, strength, and intelligence. And she was determined to become the grand duchess of Russia.

One night in 1744, during a feast celebrating the New Year, a messenger from Berlin burst in with a packet of letters. Among them was one marked "Personal! Very urgent!

SOPHIE WAS SMART and well-read. She considered herself very qualified to marry Peter, the young heir to the Russian throne.

To the Very High and Well-Born Princess Johanna Elizabeth of Anhalt-Zerbst, in her Castle of Zerbst."

Sophie's chance had arrived. She had been summoned to Russia to be judged by its empress.

Princess Johanna had gotten her wish. After all these years, the door to the highest royal circles had swung open. Sophie's father, however, wished it had stayed shut. In the parlors of Western Europe, Russia had a reputation as a violent, illiterate, and desolate land. It was filled with uneducated serfs who worked like slaves for the nobility. Even well-born Russians were said to be crude and ignorant of the current ideas and fashions in the rest of Europe. They also practiced a form of Christianity known as Russian Orthodoxy. To a devout Protestant like Sophie's father, they might as well have had no religion at all.

Prince Christian August also worried for his daughter's safety. In just over a decade, there had been three bloody takeovers of the Russian throne. Empress Elizabeth was said to be violent and unpredictable. Rumor had it she had cut out the tongue of a beautiful countess and banished her to Siberia, simply because the woman was prettier than Elizabeth. And hadn't she sent another German princess, little Ivan's mother, to prison?

Sophie must have shared some of her father's concerns. But, like her mother, she hungered for power.

She wanted to marry Peter, and felt confident that she deserved the privilege. She began a diary to record her thoughts. "Of all the matches proposed," she wrote, "I am the most brilliant."

The preparations for the journey only added to Prince Christian's anxiety. Empress Elizabeth had ordered that the trip take place under great secrecy. There were powerful people in Russia who did not want to see Elizabeth form an alliance with King Frederick and Prussia. Sophie's life could well be in danger. Elizabeth commanded Sophie and Princess Johanna to take just a handful of servants. Sophie's father would have to stay home.

The elderly prince of Anhalt-Zerbst rode with his wife and daughter as far as Berlin. He made Sophie promise not to convert to Russian Orthodoxy. She agreed, even though she doubted it was a promise she could keep. Marriage to Peter would mean adopting Russian ways. It also meant that she would probably never see her father again.

CHAPTER 3

A Heavy Crown

Princess Sophie becomes GRAND DUCHESS CATHERINE ALEXEYEVNA.

SOPHIE AND PRINCESS JOHANNA REACHED St. Petersburg in early February after many weeks of traveling through deep snow. The city gave Sophie her first taste of the exotic country that she hoped would become her home. In the Russian capital, log cabins stood in the shadows of palaces and cathedrals. Wolves and bears roamed the streets at night. Fires and floods were common. Still, Sophie had never seen such a large and rapidly growing city.

SOPHIE AND HER MOTHER traveled from Berlin to St.
Petersburg by sleigh. During this journey, they may have crossed
paths with young Tsar Ivan VI, who was being taken to a dungeon.

She arrived exhausted, only to learn that Empress
Elizabeth and Grand Duke Peter were in Moscow, 400
miles to the south.

Sophie and Johanna raced on and arrived just
in time for Peter's sixteenth-birthday celebration.
Sophie had barely removed her traveling furs when
the grand duke appeared to escort her to the empress.
Sophie noticed how puny and pale he looked but
there was no time to worry about that now. Hundreds

29

of onlookers filled the court. Their eyes scoured the German princess as she passed through the grandly decorated rooms. The procession stopped before a tall set of doors.

When the doors opened, there stood Her Imperial Majesty, the Empress Elizabeth. How beautiful she looked! She wore a shimmering, gold-trimmed silver

ELIZABETH HAD BECOME empress of Russia by overthrowing her infant cousin. She was considered to be intelligent, treacherous, and vain.

gown. Diamonds sparkled in her hair. Rumor had it that she owned 15,000 French-designed dresses and 5,000 pairs of shoes. This was the woman who controlled Sophie's future.

Elizabeth invited Sophie and Princess Johanna into her chambers. She embraced Johanna and scrutinized Sophie. Sophie curtsied carefully. When she rose, the empress kissed her. Sophie had passed her first test.

That night, Sophie and Johanna dined with Peter. Sophie couldn't believe how childish he was. He talked endlessly about soldiers and army drills. And he didn't seem at all interested in her.

After Peter's grand birthday celebration, Sophie settled into life at court. She and Peter spent their evenings together, and Sophie pleased him by playing with his toy armies. Privately, though, she was puzzled by the grand duke's behavior. French was the language at court, yet Peter stubbornly spoke German. He offended everyone around him by wearing a Prussian army uniform—his badge of loyalty to King Frederick II.

This in particular shocked Sophie. Peter was new to Russia, just as she was. Flaunting his German heritage was no way for him to win over the Russian people. Not only that, Peter mocked his new Orthodox faith. He often talked and joked during the long religious ceremonies.

By contrast, Sophie tried dutifully to learn the ways of her new country. She studied Russian culture, language, and religion from a tutor. She worked late into the night, learning to recite Orthodox prayers in Russian.

The long hours of study, the new climate, and her attempts to befriend Peter soon wore Sophie down. She caught a high fever and almost died. Empress Elizabeth herself nursed Sophie back to health. Sophie's dedication to all things Russian had endeared her to the empress. By the summer, Elizabeth had decided that Sophie and Peter would marry.

In June 1744, Sophie completed her transformation. Despite her father's plea, she converted to the Russian Orthodox faith. She fasted for three days to prepare for the ceremony. Then she knelt in the palace chapel and recited the Russian prayers she had memorized. Elizabeth was so moved that she wept. When the ceremony was over, Princess Sophie was re-christened. From now on, she would be known as Catherine Alexeyevna, or Catherine.

There was no going back now. Sophie, now Catherine, was married to Peter on August 21, 1745, and became the Grand Duchess of All of the Russias. The St. Petersburg wedding was the most expensive Russia had ever seen. Huge crowds lined the streets as the couple rode in a jeweled coach to Kazan Cathedral, escorted by 120 carriages.

The wedding was exhausting. Catherine held stiff and straight through three hours of prayers and sermons, burdened with an enormous crown and a gown that weighed nearly half as much as she did. That night she waited and waited in her chambers for Peter. But Peter stayed out late drinking with his guardsmen. He had already announced to Catherine that he didn't love her.

CATHERINE WON OVER the empress and married Peter. It was not a match made in heaven. He declared that he didn't love her, and she was disgusted by his immaturity.

PART 2

Grand Duchess Catherine Alexeyevna

CHAPTER 4

❦❦❦❦❦❦❦❦❦❦❦❦❦❦

Watch Your Step

Imprisoned in luxury,
Catherine learns to survive
IN THE TREACHEROUS
RUSSIAN COURT.

CATHERINE'S NEW LIFE AS GRAND
duchess bustled with activity. She was constantly
surrounded by people at the court in St. Petersburg.
Ladies-in-waiting fawned over her. She danced at
formal balls and sat through official dinners with
foreign diplomats.

But her life as grand duchess grew increasingly
lonely. Peter treated her coldly and cruelly. On some

days he made Catherine dress like a soldier and stand guard outside his room for hours. Once, Peter showed Catherine a dead pet rat that he had hung by its neck for being a "bad soldier." Most humiliating of all, Peter drank heavily and chased after the ladies at court.

CATHERINE'S HUSBAND, PETER, was obsessed with the military. But he had more experience playing with toy soldiers than fighting in real combat. He also alienated Russians with his loyalty to Russia's archenemy, Prussia.

Catherine did not dare to complain about Peter's behavior. If she displeased him, Peter said, he would divorce her and have her banished to a convent, where she would live like a nun.

Empress Elizabeth, too, turned against Catherine. Now that Catherine had married into the family, she posed a danger to the empress. How could Elizabeth be sure that her adopted son and his young wife weren't plotting to seize the throne from her? Elizabeth confined Catherine to a suite of rooms and surrounded her with spies. If Catherine made friends with her ladies-in-waiting, Elizabeth sent them away.

Before long, the empress took away Catherine's last source of emotional support. Elizabeth had never trusted the scheming, striving Princess Johanna. Now she found evidence to back up her suspicions. Elizabeth caught Johanna writing secret letters to King Frederick II in Berlin, informing the Prussian ruler about the politics of the Russian court. Elizabeth ordered Johanna to leave Russia and never return.

Catherine watched while her mother's coach left for the long return journey to Stettin. Now she felt completely alone, a prisoner in an unfriendly land. On the empress's orders, she could not even write letters home.

To survive, Catherine turned to her writing and reading. She read history and poetry. She kept up with the scientific discoveries of the day. Most of all, she loved philosophy. It wasn't long before she discovered the ideas of a revolutionary new movement known as the Enlightenment.

Catherine devoured the writings of the men who led the movement—the French writers Denis Diderot, Voltaire, and Jean Jacques Rousseau. These philosophers caused great controversy in France. They challenged the right of the Roman Catholic Church to control people's lives. They advocated freedom of speech. They insisted that kings and queens had to respect the will of their people and govern by a system of laws rather than by their own whims. Their writings placed them in constant danger of being censored, jailed, or exiled.

Catherine absorbed the ideas of the Enlightenment with great interest. After all, her incompetent husband would one day be tsar of Russia, and Catherine would rule by his side. When the time came, she wanted to rule wisely.

The seasons passed slowly as Catherine prepared for her future. In the summer, Empress Elizabeth took her entire court on the road, traveling from town to town. The rest of the year, she moved back and forth between St. Petersburg and Moscow, dragging Catherine and Peter with her.

Catherine did what she could to adjust to her new life. She loved spending time outdoors. She grew strong from hunting and horseback riding. She had a special saddle made that allowed her to sit both sidesaddle, as most women did, or astride, the way men rode. By the time she turned 23, Catherine was not only well educated; she had grown healthy and pretty.

LOCATED IN THE HEART of Moscow, the Kremlin fortress had been home to Russian tsars for centuries. For Catherine, life there was dull; her fellow nobles seemed to be interested only in food, drink, and gossip.

Still, Catherine struggled to feel at home. She found the Russian nobility crude and boring. Dressed in their best French fashions, they spat on floors and let garbage pile up in their fancy homes. Few nobles read books or talked about ideas. How the young duchess longed for a bright mind to match her own!

One night at a party in the grand Summer Palace in St. Petersburg, Catherine spotted a handsome, dark-eyed man across the room. His name was Sergei

Saltykov, and he served as a high-ranking official in the royal household. He had a charming smile and a gift for flattery. He also had his heart set on winning the affection of the grand duchess.

Soon, the dashing Saltykov appeared by Catherine's side at parties and dances. Catherine felt her loneliness melt. Several months later, she was pregnant. Rumors swirled through the court about who the father was.

NEGLECTED BY HER HUSBAND, PETER, Catherine fell in love with Count Saltykov (at left).

CHAPTER 5

An Heir Is Born

Catherine bears a son and
GATHERS HER COURAGE.

IN SEPTEMBER 1754, CATHERINE LAY DAYS away from producing an heir to the Russian throne. Empress Elizabeth had decided to ignore the whispers about the child's paternity. She brought Catherine into her own suite and confined her to a stark and dreary birth chamber. Catherine confided to her diary that she felt "wretched as a stone." But having the child was her duty, and she didn't complain aloud.

On September 19, Catherine went into a long and painful labor. She suffered all night on a hard cot while

Elizabeth prayed over her and the midwife fretted. At last her son was born. Catherine reached for her baby, but the midwife snatched him away and handed him to the empress. Elizabeth named the boy Paul Petrovich and swept him out of the room.

In the streets of St. Petersburg, hundreds of cathedral bells rang out, announcing Paul's birth. Inside the palace, no one visited Catherine. She caught a dangerous fever and spent hours weeping. It was six weeks before she was allowed a quick look at her baby boy. She thought he was beautiful, but the small glimpse made the separation harder than ever. She wasn't allowed to attend Paul's baptism and had to bribe servants for news about his health. To keep her sanity, Catherine returned to her reading and writing.

A freezing winter set in. While Peter drank at night with his guardsman friends, Catherine holed up in a drafty room and plotted her revenge. In her ten years at court, she had observed that Elizabeth did not involve herself in the details of government. Catherine

A BAPTISM IN RUSSIA in the 1700s. Empress Elizabeth did
not allow Catherine to attend the baptism of Catherine's
first son, Paul Petrovich.

vowed that if she became empress, she would not make
the same mistake. As soon as she recovered her health,
she meant to seek out influential friends and make her
voice heard in the political debates of the day.

Catherine chose Peter's 27th-birthday celebration to
make her new debut at court. She wore a blue velvet
gown that complimented her tall, slim figure and made
her look regal. She strode into the party—and back
into public life—with her head held high. She ignored

some important people and fawned over others. Her entrance was carefully calculated, and it made everyone take notice. The foreign diplomats were impressed. They began to realize that Catherine could become a very powerful woman.

One such diplomat was Sir Charles Hanbury-Williams, who had arrived that year from Great Britain with an important mission. King Frederick II was once again stirring up trouble in Europe. The British were allied with Prussia, and wanted Russia on their side if a war were to start.

Hanbury-Williams admired Catherine and thought she held the future of Russia in her hands. Behind Elizabeth's back, Catherine and Hanbury-Williams became friends and allies. Catherine gave Hanbury-Williams secret information for Britain. In return, she received large amounts of money, which she used to bribe informants for more court secrets.

Hanbury-Williams did Catherine another favor as well. He introduced her to a romantic young Polish count, Stanislas Poniatowski. It was no secret that Peter had taken a mistress—a woman whom Catherine considered crude and silly. So when the worldly and artistic Polish count arrived in Catherine's life, she welcomed his affections.

IN 1755, CATHERINE EMERGED as a serious
political force. She schemed with British diplomats and
romanced foreign nobles.

CHAPTER 6

Accused of Treason

Catherine has a SHOWDOWN WITH EMPRESS ELIZABETH.

IN 1756, KING FREDERICK II AND HIS fearsome Prussian army invaded Austrian territory, sweeping most of Europe into history's first worldwide war. Great Britain sided with Prussia. Elizabeth threw Russia's support behind Austria and France. The Seven Years' War had begun.

Catherine had chosen a dangerous time to be friends with a British diplomat. The Russian court simmered with rumors of treachery. Catherine's friend Hanbury-Williams was sent home after Elizabeth rejected his plea for aid. Russian troops then marched into East Prussia to help battle the mighty army of Catherine's former patron, King Frederick II.

Empress Elizabeth was now in her late forties. She had grown even more suspicious with age. She was

KING FREDERICK II AND HIS PRUSSIAN TROOPS in battle against the Austrians during the Seven Years' War. Elizabeth had allied Russia with Austria, but Catherine was conspiring with Prussia's British allies.

so afraid of being assassinated in her sleep that she moved to a new room each night. Her spies prowled St. Petersburg and Moscow, looking for conspiracies. By making political friendships, Catherine was playing with fire.

In addition to Hanbury-Williams, Catherine courted other powerful friends. One of them was Elizabeth's chancellor, Alexei Bestuzhev. Bestuzhev managed Russia's foreign policy, and like Hanbury-Williams, he believed that Catherine would soon come to power in Russia. He and Catherine began writing letters to one another in secret, discussing Russia's involvement in the war and Catherine's role in Russia's future. Bestuzhev had proposed a plan by which Catherine would become empress upon Elizabeth's death, and he would control most of the important government offices.

When rumors of these letters reached Elizabeth, the empress grew furious with her daughter-in-law. Catherine was saved only by a stroke of fate—she was pregnant again. Court gossip hinted that the

CATHERINE'S FRIEND, Chancellor Bestuzhev, thought Russia was on the wrong side of the Seven Years' War. Elizabeth had him exiled.

Polish Count Poniatowski was the father, but once again Elizabeth did not acknowledge the rumors. And Catherine could not be imprisoned while carrying a possible heir to the throne.

In December 1757, Catherine gave birth to a baby girl. Hoping to please Elizabeth, she asked to name the baby after her. The empress refused to be flattered. She named the child Anna after Peter's mother and carried the baby off to her rooms. In the following weeks, Catherine hid in her chambers, fearing for her life. Now that the baby was born, would Elizabeth send her into exile—or worse, condemn her to prison or even death?

In February 1758, the crisis deepened when Bestuzhev was arrested and charged with treason.

Catherine received a secret message from the disgraced chancellor assuring her that he had burned all their correspondence. Still, she felt she had to act. She wrote to Elizabeth requesting a meeting.

Catherine waited anxiously for two months. Finally she was summoned to Elizabeth's apartments. It was the dead of night. The empress, who had trouble sleeping, often conducted her business in these dreary hours.

Catherine entered the huge, cold, dimly lit room and realized that her day of judgment had arrived. Peter stood beside the empress, smirking. Catherine could hear breathing from behind a screen set up in the shadows: A judge sat in hiding to witness her downfall. Catherine was suspected of committing treason, and this was to be her trial.

Catherine thought quickly. Her only hope was to appeal to the empress's emotions. She threw herself at Elizabeth's feet. She confessed that she had reached the depths of despair. How lonely she was, how unloved!

"Send me home," she begged. "My children are in your hands! I hope you will not abandon them!"

The old woman softened for a moment but quickly returned to the task at hand. "You have meddled in many things which have nothing to do with you," she told Catherine.

Catherine begged forgiveness, but insisted that she had never done anything disloyal.

Peter could barely contain himself. Here was his chance to get rid of his wife so he could marry his mistress, and he did not want to see it slip away. Throughout the interrogation, he interrupted angrily, trying to convince Elizabeth that Catherine was lying. His outbursts only seemed to annoy the empress.

Angered by Peter and touched by Catherine's apologies, Elizabeth finally decided to end her daughter-in-law's misery. She dismissed Catherine and sent an aide after her to tell her "not to be distressed."

With a timely performance, Catherine had won the empress's trust—and perhaps saved her own life.

Changing of the Guard

CATHERINE WINS SOME POWERFUL FRIENDS
and loses a mother-in-law.

THREE YEARS AFTER CATHERINE'S TRUCE with the empress, Elizabeth grew ill, raising once again the question of who would rule Russia after her death. Peter was next in line to become tsar, but his behavior had convinced many people that he was unfit to rule. In 1760, Russian and Austrian troops had rolled into Berlin, only to be turned back by the Prussian army. Peter openly celebrated the Prussian victory. He called King Frederick II his "master," infuriating his own Russian guardsmen.

Catherine quickly distanced herself from her husband. She made it known that despite her German birth, she supported Russia with all her heart. Her loyal backing for the war effort earned her the respect of some powerful members of the Imperial Guard. Their support, she knew, could be crucial in the future.

One of these guardsmen stood out above the rest, an artillery officer named Gregory Orlov. Orlov was a giant of a man, rock solid and fearless. Legend had it that in one fiery battle with the Prussians he was wounded three times, but each time he rose up to defend his men.

Catherine first saw Orlov from a palace window. She found him handsome and dashing—not to mention potentially useful. A few weeks later, their romance began.

Orlov had three brothers in the Imperial Guard. Strong and ambitious, the brothers commanded the loyalty of hundreds of soldiers. And they adored Catherine. They let it be known that they were ready to give their lives for her.

By December 1761, Empress Elizabeth lay near death. People at court were desperate to know who

GREGORY ORLOV (LEFT) AND HIS BROTHER ALEXIS
were two high-ranking officers in the Imperial Guard. Like
most Russian soldiers, they hated Peter. Catherine sensed an
opportunity and allied with them.

the next ruler would be. Elizabeth had not named a successor. Would Peter be able to seize power? Would Catherine? Or would another leader rise up and launch a palace coup?

Catherine had decided by now that she could not survive as Peter's obedient wife. She wrote in her diary that her choice was clear. She could support Peter and perish with him. Or she could attempt to save herself, her son, and Russia from the "shipwreck" that her husband would certainly create.

For now, however, Catherine was in no position to play the savior. Once again she was pregnant, this time with Gregory Orlov's child. She had been careful to hide her condition from all but a trusted few. If Peter found out, he could announce to the world that Catherine had committed adultery and use her disgrace as the excuse he needed to send her away.

On January 3, 1762, Catherine and Peter were summoned to the empress's bedchamber. Catherine stood by the bed, where Elizabeth was surrounded by burning candles, priests, black-robed monks, and ladies-in-waiting. As she whispered the prayer for the dying, Catherine was overcome. Here was the woman she had so revered and feared, at the end of her life. Catherine fell to her knees and wept.

On January 5, 1762, bells rang out across St. Petersburg, announcing the news that an important Prussian fortress had fallen to Russia. The war was all but won. In the palace, Catherine and Peter waited outside Elizabeth's chambers. Finally, at four in the afternoon, the doors opened and the announcement was made: "Her Imperial Majesty has fallen asleep in the Lord. God preserve our gracious sovereign, Emperor Peter the Third."

Outside the palace, soldiers loyal to Peter gathered to protect the new emperor from any challenge to his throne. In Elizabeth's chambers, those assembled fell to their knees before Peter and crossed themselves. They prayed for the dead empress and for their new ruler.

Catherine stood quietly beside the body of the empress, apparently overlooked by everyone.

CHAPTER 8

The Emperor's New Clothes

PETER MAKES ENEMIES
of church and state.

For weeks, while all of Russia mourned Elizabeth's death, the body of the empress lay on display in the Kazan Cathedral. Catherine hid her pregnancy under a heavy black dress and prayed for hours beside the coffin. The stench that rose from Elizabeth's preserved body was horrible, but to move away was a sign of disrespect. Only the priests' incense kept Catherine from gagging.

CATHERINE MOURNS the death of Elizabeth. Her show of respect for the dead empress gained her the loyalty of many Russians.

Catherine's devotion won her respect from both the nobles at court and the serfs in the countryside. Peter, by contrast, seemed determined to disgrace himself. He rarely came to the cathedral in the weeks after his adoptive mother's death. He was too busy holding parties and flirting with the ladies at court. When he did visit Elizabeth's body, he refused to wear black or pray.

Instead his laughter rang out over the stones, and his jokes made everyone wince.

In the early weeks of Peter's reign, Catherine stayed out of her husband's way. She simply watched while he made enemies right and left.

Peter's first important act as tsar alienated most of the Russian military. He appeared publicly in a Prussian army uniform and demanded that his soldiers do the same. Then, with the Russian army nearing victory in Prussia, Peter signed a treaty with King Frederick II and gave back the land the Russian army had fought so hard to win. To many Russians, the treaty seemed more than foolish—it was treason!

While the military seethed, Peter attacked another cherished institution—the Russian Orthodox Church. He took over church property and sent soldiers to demand payments from priests and bishops. He also tried to force Western practices on Russian worshippers. He supposedly told church leaders to remove icons— sacred paintings of saints—from local churches. He

PETER WITH THE KING OF SWEDEN AND KING
FREDERICK II OF PRUSSIA. Peter (right) worshipped Frederick
(center), and when Peter became tsar, he returned all the lands
that the Russian army had seized from Prussia.

tried to force priests to shave their beards and shed their
long black robes in favor of the trim coats and shirts
worn by Western priests.

Russia rumbled with anger as news of Peter's
treachery spread. Guardsmen grumbled in their

barracks, encouraged by the Orlovs. In St. Petersburg and Moscow, the faithful protested the attacks on their church.

In April, the time came for Catherine to give birth. She had to be careful. If her pregnancy became known to the royal court, Peter would have an easy excuse to divorce her. So she hatched a plan with a trusted valet. On April 11, 1762, as Catherine gave birth, the valet set a fire outside the palace to distract unfriendly ears and eyes.

The plan worked. Peter, who loved fires, rushed to the scene with his courtiers. Back at the palace, Catherine brought another son into the world.

Little Alexis Grigoryevich was bundled up and sent to the countryside, where he would be raised in secrecy by one of Catherine's trusted servants. A scandal had been averted. And Catherine's last obstacle to seizing the throne was removed.

CHAPTER 9

The Coup

Catherine seizes
THE THRONE AT LAST.

BY THE SUMMER OF 1762, CATHERINE HAD laid plans to overthrow her husband, Tsar Peter III of Russia. Gregory Orlov had been secretly using the Imperial Guard's treasury to bribe soldiers to support their cause. Catherine had secured a promise of aid from Great Britain.

Catherine took up residence in the royal summerhouse at Peterhof, where she waited anxiously for the next move. Either Gregory Orlov would signal that the time was right, or Peter would find out about the plot and throw his disloyal wife into a dungeon.

On June 28, 1762, Catherine was woken at dawn by Alexis Orlov, Gregory's scar-faced brother. One of Gregory's lieutenants had been arrested after spies overheard him speaking against the tsar. Alexis feared that the lieutenant would be tortured until he revealed the plot. Peter was at the royal estate in Oranienbaum, just outside of St. Petersburg, but there was no telling when he might hear of the arrest. "We must go!" Alexis said. "Everything is ready to proclaim you empress!"

Catherine leaped up and raced by carriage to St. Petersburg. She came to a halt at a barracks of the palace guard, where royal guardsmen were waiting in formation. Their drums rolled as Catherine stepped out of her carriage. Gregory Orlov paraded past the guardsmen on horseback. He stood in his stirrups and raised his sword. "Hurrah for our Little Mother Catherine!" he cried.

The officers of the guard knelt to kiss Catherine's cloak and swear their allegiance. A roar went up.

Catherine was heralded as Her Majesty the Empress of all Russia.

Now Catherine had guards lead her to the next barracks, and the next. As she advanced, thousands joined the march. The streets of St. Petersburg filled with crowds shouting her name. Sabers were raised and cries of "Catherine! Our Little Mother Catherine!" filled the air. Joyfully, Catherine made her way to Kazan Cathedral, where an archbishop proclaimed her empress in the eyes of the Orthodox Church.

Then she rode to the Winter Palace. While her loyal troops, now 40,000 strong, secured the palace, Catherine sent messengers into the countryside with an announcement for all to hear. Her husband had "betrayed" the country and its people. She, the new empress of Russia, had seized the throne in order to save the church and protect the security of the empire.

With the country put on notice, Catherine turned her attention to Peter, who still commanded the loyalty of 1,000 troops at Oranienbaum. Dressed in a uniform

SOLDIERS CHEER AS CATHERINE (on horseback and wearing a military uniform) proclaims herself the empress of Russia. As soon as she put her coup into motion, 40,000 soldiers joined her cause.

TSAR PETER III IS MURDERED by Alexis Orlov, probably
by the order of Catherine. Peter had given up his throne
without a fight, but the new empress feared he would be a
threat to her crown for as long as he lived.

of the Imperial Guard, she made her appearance on the palace steps. As she leaped onto her horse, a handsome young guard came forward to offer the tassel from his sword. His name was Gregory Potemkin. Later, she would remember his blazing face.

It wasn't long before Peter received news of the coup. He reportedly turned to his mistress and spat out, "What did I tell you? That woman is capable of anything!"

Faced with massive defections among his troops, Peter simply gave up the throne to his wife. Catherine had him separated from his mistress. She imprisoned him in a summer home near St. Petersburg. Peter begged to be released to another country, but Catherine knew that as long as he lived, her position was threatened.

A few weeks later, the secret letter from Alexis Orlov reached Catherine's desk. Peter was dead. Catherine stood alone as the empress of mighty Russia.

Catherine the Great in Pictures

SMALL-TOWN PRINCESS

Catherine was born Princess Sophie of Anhalt-Zerbst. Her father was a minor prince who governed a seaport on the outskirts of Prussia.

UNFIT HUSBAND

When she was 15, Sophie became engaged to Peter and changed her name to Catherine. Peter was the heir to the Russian throne. He was also immature and cruel.

FLAWED TSARINA

Empress Elizabeth of Russia was intelligent, but she was also vain and treacherous. She spent more time spending money than she did governing her empire.

WILD CAPITAL

St. Petersburg, the brand-new capital of Russia, was founded by Elizabeth's father, Tsar Peter the Great. Streets were lined with grand palaces, but bears and other wildlife still roamed at night.

ROYAL DIVORCE

In 1762, Catherine led thousands of rebellious troops to overthrow her husband. Peter surrendered without a fight, and Catherine became empress of Russia.

MURDER OF A TSAR

Peter was assassinated by Alexis Orlov, the brother of Catherine's lover. Peter had renounced his throne, but there was always a chance that disloyal nobles would rally around him.

SYMBOL OF POWER

In 1762, Catherine was crowned
Empress Catherine II. This crown,
which contains nearly 5,000
diamonds, was made for
her coronation.

ENLIGHTENED EMPRESS

Catherine was 33 years old
when she became empress.
She planned to modernize
Russia and give its people
more rights.

A WORKHORSE

Unlike Elizabeth, Catherine worked
hard and was very involved in
government matters.

URBAN POOR
Starving Russians beg for money in St. Petersburg. When Catherine took the throne, Russia was one of the poorest nations in Europe.

TREASURES OF THE WEST
Catherine loved the artwork of the West. In 1764, she bought 255 paintings for her new private gallery, the Hermitage.

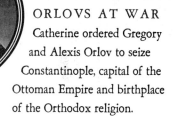

ORLOVS AT WAR
Catherine ordered Gregory and Alexis Orlov to seize Constantinople, capital of the Ottoman Empire and birthplace of the Orthodox religion.

TRIUMPH AT SEA
Led by Alexis Orlov, the Russian navy massacred an Ottoman fleet. Catherine was never able to capture Constantinople.

BACK FROM THE DEAD?

Claiming to be Catherine's dead husband, Emilian Pugachev tried to conquer Moscow with an army of Cossacks and starving serfs.

A NEW CHAMPION

Gregory Potemkin helped the empress crush Pugachev's rebellion. In 1783, Potemkin then led an army into the Crimea, a rich land with ports on the Black Sea. He also became the love of Catherine's life.

CRIMEAN COVER-UP

In 1787, Potemkin organized a tour of the Crimea for Catherine and the rulers of Austria and Poland. Critics claimed that Potemkin covered up the region's poverty with fake villages and smiling actors.

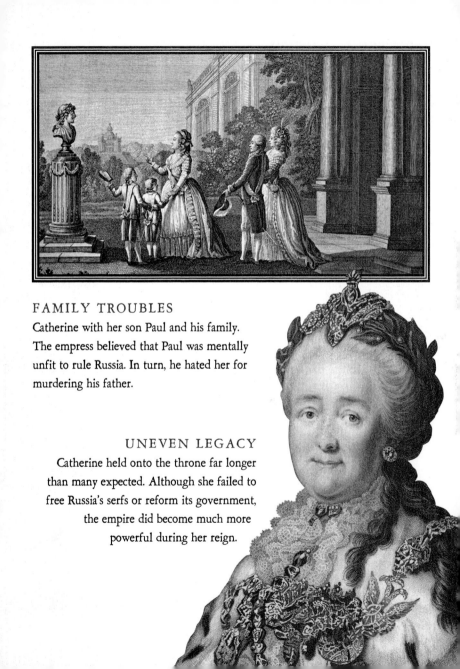

FAMILY TROUBLES

Catherine with her son Paul and his family. The empress believed that Paul was mentally unfit to rule Russia. In turn, he hated her for murdering his father.

UNEVEN LEGACY

Catherine held onto the throne far longer than many expected. Although she failed to free Russia's serfs or reform its government, the empire did become much more powerful during her reign.

PART 3

Catherine, Empress of Russia

Down to Business

Catherine takes CONTROL OF AN EMPIRE.

AT THE AGE OF 33, CATHERINE FINALLY had what she had worked so hard to attain: power. Now, she felt great pressure to use it wisely.

Russia had been ravaged by years of war and mismanagement. The treasury was empty. Floods and crop failures had left thousands of people starving in the countryside. Desperate serfs rebelled against their landowners. Soldiers who had not been paid in weeks threatened to revolt against their officers.

IN SEPTEMBER 1762, Catherine was officially crowned Empress Catherine II at the Kremlin in Moscow. She was 33. Outsiders doubted that she had the skill or strength to hold onto the throne.

In the early months of her reign, Catherine received little support at home or abroad. The nobles of St. Petersburg and Moscow resented the fact that their new empress was not descended from Russian royalty. Soldiers in the barracks grew jealous of the Orlovs' influence over the empress. And millions of Russian peasants who remained loyal to Peter blamed Catherine for his murder.

Foreign observers were equally harsh about the new empress. Newspapers in Great Britain and France used Peter's death to paint Catherine as yet another brutal ruler of Russia's violent empire. Most people expected Catherine, like many Russian rulers before her, to be overthrown at any moment. She was, after all, a woman with a shaky claim to the throne and no husband to back up her authority.

But Catherine was no weakling. She had spent years waiting for her chance to seize the throne and had no intention of losing her grip. She ignored her

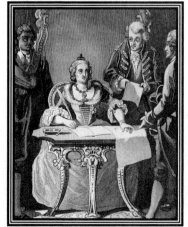

critics and got to work. Each morning, she rose at six to read and write for two hours. Then she

CATHERINE AT HER DESK, surrounded by her officials. Elizabeth had used the throne to enhance her personal glory. Peter treated it like a plaything. Catherine was determined to avoid their mistakes.

began a day of work that often lasted until 11 at night. She reviewed and signed official documents. She received an endless stream of office-seekers, advisers, and bureaucrats and took their pleas seriously. She took a personal interest in everything from the price of grain to the quality of Russia's insane asylums. Most importantly, she set out to remake Russia in the image of the Enlightenment thinkers she so admired.

Catherine vowed to bring her sprawling empire into the modern age. She converted a convent into a school for girls, the first of its kind in Russia. She built hospitals and urged the use of modern science to treat patients. She founded an art museum called the Hermitage and began stocking it with treasures from Western Europe.

She planned a system of laws meant to provide equal treatment to people throughout the country. In 1767, she published a guide for future lawmakers called the *Great Instruction.* In it, she called for freedom of speech and of the press, argued against the death penalty, and insisted that the rich be prevented from oppressing the poor.

King Louis XV of France considered the document so threatening that he banned it throughout his realm.

Eager to let the world know about her reforms, Catherine began writing open letters to the famous French philosophers who had inspired her. She praised Voltaire for fighting against "the massed enemies of mankind: superstition, fanaticism, ignorance . . . and the abuse of power." Flattered, Voltaire told Catherine she was "the brightest star of the north."

Catherine wrote to Denis Diderot, who was

CATHERINE BUILT the Hermitage to be a private gallery for her personal collection of Western art. The empress was fascinated by the culture of the West and wanted to pattern Russia after its philosophical, scientific, and artistic ideals.

struggling to finish a controversial collection of writings called the *Encyclopedia*. The vast project included all the new ideas of the time. Like Catherine's own *Great Instruction*, it had been banned in France. Catherine invited Diderot to Russia, where he could complete his work in peace.

Catherine did her best to convince the world that her Russia would be different from the old Russia. Despite threats on her life, she traveled through the streets of St. Petersburg in an open carriage. She held concerts, plays, and ballets and required her courtiers to take part. She appeared at lavish balls and treated everyone with kindness and grace. Her Russia would be a place where new ideas could be discussed openly, where people were governed by laws rather than the whims of an empress and her henchmen.

Behind the shiny image, however, Catherine had trouble living up to her own ideals. Enemies lurked around every corner, and Catherine moved quickly to silence them. Just ten days after she became empress,

CATHERINE WAS A CHARMING, open-minded, and dedicated ruler. But she also had a dark side. One of her first acts as empress was to revive the secret police. These spies combed the empire looking for disloyal Russians to arrest and torture.

she revived a police agency known as the Secret Branch. Its mission was to uncover conspiracies against the crown, and its agents did their work ruthlessly. They tortured several soldiers until they admitted plotting to overthrow Catherine. The soldiers were exiled to Siberia. They overheard a couple of chambermaids joking that Catherine acted like a man. The girls were promptly banished from court. They discovered a group of nobles grumbling that Orlov—a common soldier—was the true power behind the throne. The nobles, too, were sent into exile.

In July 1764, a more serious plot fell apart as it unfolded. A young officer tried to rescue the former tsar, Ivan VI, from prison in order to place him on the throne. Under orders from Catherine, guards killed Ivan. The officer was executed as well, but people whispered that Catherine had framed him so that she could murder yet another tsar.

After several years as empress, Catherine was far from content. She had power and a vision for her country. But she struggled to impose her will on her reluctant subjects. She had a dashing and powerful companion in Gregory Orlov. But she could not marry him without risking a revolt by the soldiers who hated the Orlovs or the nobles who felt she should marry someone of royal blood.

It was time, perhaps, to look beyond the borders of Russia for the glory worthy of an empress. It was time to go to war.

A ROYAL GUINEA PIG

EVERY YEAR, SMALLPOX KILLED THOUSANDS of Russian children, and traditional medicine could do nothing to stop the disease. Catherine thought that modern science had the answer—and she was willing to bet her life on it.

She had read a British book on a new treatment known as vaccination. Few people believed it would work. How could putting germs in your body fight off a disease?

Ignoring the doubters, Catherine invited the author of the book, Dr. Thomas Dimsdale, to Russia. Dimsdale injected the empress with pus from a small-pox victim.

The court waited nervously as Catherine developed pustules and a sore throat. But the disease went no further—the experiment was a success. In a brave attempt to modernize Russia, Catherine had risked her life.

SMALLPOX PUSTULES. Smallpox killed one-third of its victims.

A New World Power

Catherine challenges the Ottoman Empire and TAKES A NEW PLACE ON THE WORLD STAGE.

CATHERINE CRAVED ADMIRATION FOR her new ideas. She also wanted respect for the raw power of the Russian military. In the presence of foreign diplomats, she referred often to her "great and powerful empire." But she had yet to prove just how powerful it was.

First she turned south, to the Ottoman Empire.

The Ottoman Turks had been expanding north toward Russia for some 500 years. In 1453, they seized the city of Constantinople, the ancient home of the Orthodox faith. They converted Christian Orthodox churches into Muslim mosques and made the city their capital.

Catherine wanted to push the Turks out of Europe—though her motives were as much economic as they were religious. The Turks controlled the Crimea, a rich land on the coast of the Black Sea, just 700 miles south of Moscow. If Catherine could seize the Crimea, Russia would have its first warm-water ports.

Few observers gave Russia any chance of winning a war against the Ottoman Empire. Catherine's armies were disorganized, poorly armed, and under-supplied. Turkish forces outnumbered them three to one. And Catherine had never faced a war as a ruler.

But the empress seemed to relish the challenge. In 1768, she provoked a conflict by sending a Russian regiment across the border into Turkish land. The sultan of the Ottoman Empire, Mustafa III, declared war on Russia. With Gregory Orlov planning the assault, Catherine decided to attack the Turks by land and sea.

In September 1769, her armies crossed the border into the Crimea. They captured the key cities of Azov and Taganrog. Less than a year later, an army of 17,000 Russians demoralized 150,000 Turks on the River Kagul.

Meanwhile, Russian warships sailed from the Baltic Sea into the Mediterranean. In 1770, led by Alexis Orlov, they attacked a much larger Ottoman fleet

ALEXIS ORLOV'S WARSHIPS destroy an Ottoman fleet anchored in Chesma Bay. As many as 11,000 Turkish sailors died during this battle.

that had anchored off the coast of Turkey. After a day of intense cannon fire, several Turkish ships had been sunk. The rest burned fiercely in the night air. One account claimed that 11,000 Turkish sailors were drowned.

Alexis's victory in the Mediterranean Sea put the Russians in command of the war. Catherine was in awe of her country's military might. She wrote to Voltaire to tell him the battle had killed so many Turks that the water turned red with blood. "War is a wretched business!" she said.

But in fact, Catherine could barely contain her joy. She had embarrassed the French king, who had supported the Turks. Her navy had impressed the British, whose powerful fleet ruled the seas. Catherine had proven herself a war leader and earned Russia the respect and status of a world power.

"The Turks," she gloated in her diary, "have taken it into their heads to waken the sleeping cat . . . and now the cat is going to run after the mice."

CHAPTER 12

The Breakup

With discontent rising in both
city and country, Catherine decides
IT'S TIME FOR A CHANGE.

THE TURKISH WAR DRAGGED ON FOR
years following Alexis Orlov's grand triumph at sea.
The Russian people were paying a high price to keep
the war going. Thousands of soldiers died every month
and had to be replaced by reluctant serfs from the
countryside. What's more, the Russian economy was
in chaos, and prices for basic goods soared. Hungry
peasants grew frustrated with the war and angry with
their empress.

The most immediate threat to Catherine came from guardsmen who opposed the Orlovs and the ongoing war. Rumors of assassination plots leaked from army barracks in St. Petersburg and Moscow. Gregory Orlov discovered one army officer lying in wait for Catherine, a dagger in hand. In 1772, the Secret Branch uncovered a massive plot among the St. Petersburg guards. Dozens of officers in the guard, enemies of the Orlovs, had planned to overthrow Catherine and place her son Paul on the throne.

The plot was the last straw in Catherine's crumbling relationship with Gregory. For 11 years, she had ruled with Gregory at her side. But his enemies among the guard could no longer be ignored. Besides, she had grown tired of his stubborn will and his insistent advice. Just a year earlier, he had ruined peace talks with the Ottomans when he lost his temper and threatened to attack Constantinople.

Catherine had finally had enough. Gregory had become a threat to the country and the crown. Catherine sent him away and told a friend she was ready to live "according to her pleasure, and in entire independence."

While she adjusted to life without Orlov, Catherine found a happy distraction from her troubles at court. Denis Diderot, the famous French philosopher, finally accepted her ten-year-old invitation to come to Russia.

Catherine was delighted to have such a famous and brilliant man join her inner circle. They met almost

CATHERINE TALKS with the Enlightenment philosopher Denis Diderot. At first, the empress was thrilled to have such a brilliant visitor.

daily and talked for hours at a time. Diderot questioned Catherine about Russia and carefully recorded her answers. In return, he talked freely about the importance of free speech and humane government. Carried away by his own ideas, he paced the floor shouting and waving his arms. To emphasize a point, he sometimes tore off his wig and threw it across the room. "His is an extraordinary brain," Catherine wrote to Voltaire. "One does not encounter such every day."

But all the intellectual discussion in the world couldn't shield Catherine from the chaos brewing outside her palace walls. For some months, a rebellion had been sweeping toward Moscow and St. Petersburg. It had started among the Cossacks—the fierce, semi-independent horsemen who lived on the plains of southeast Russia. In October, an army of Cossacks and serfs had laid siege to the fortress town of Orenburg. They numbered 10,000 men, and their numbers were growing fast. Their leader claimed to be Catherine's dead husband, Peter III.

THE SERFS OF RUSSIA

IN CATHERINE'S TIME, MOST RUSSIANS WERE serfs—peasants who lived in conditions that were little better than slavery. Nearly seven million men and their families were forced to work lands owned by wealthy landlords or the state.

Serfs had few rights under the law. They had to hand over a portion of their crops to their landlord. They could be jailed if they tried to leave their land. Their masters could sell them to another landlord on a moment's notice. And if a master sold a serf, he had the right to keep the serf's property and his family.

When Catherine came to power, she had plans to free the serfs. But she ran into sharp resistance from the Russian nobility. The nobles were "cruel and irrational," Catherine complained, but her power depended on their loyalty. Catherine made only weak attempts to protect the serfs, and in 1773, conditions remained ripe for rebellion.

SERFS WERE OFTEN BEATEN by their landlords.

Pugachev and Potemkin

Catherine finds the love of her life and FIGHTS OFF A PRETENDER TO THE THRONE.

DURING THE WINTER OF 1773 TO 1774, A bloody rebellion swept through the south of Russia, inspired by a fiery Cossack named Emilian Pugachev. Pugachev rode from village to village with a hundred men who posed as his loyal nobles. He wore a long red robe and a nobleman's velvet cap. At each stop, he announced himself as Peter, the rightful tsar of Russia.

He had been miraculously spared from death by an act of God, he claimed. Catherine had stolen the throne from him, and he intended to take it back.

Pugachev promised food and coins to anyone who would join him. He offered rewards to serfs who rose up and killed their landlords. They joined Pugachev by the thousands, brandishing scythes, axes, and pitchforks.

Pugachev's rebels failed to seize Orenburg, so they began to move north toward Moscow. As they marched, they left a trail of murdered landlords and ransacked estates.

In the early spring of 1774, Catherine feared for her life. With Orlov gone, she had no one she could trust to help her through the crisis. Diderot was no help. He had begun to annoy her with his constant criticism. When was she going to free the "slaves" in Russia? he demanded. When was she going to make peace with the Ottomans? In her diary, Catherine complained that Diderot was just a writer who worked with paper and pen. She was an empress. She had to make real decisions that could make or break the lives of millions of people—and right now, she had to make them alone.

In the midst of Pugachev's rebellion, Catherine reached out for help. She summoned Gregory Potemkin to court. As a young soldier, Potemkin had gallantly presented the tassel from his sword to the empress during her coup. Now middle aged, he was still an impressive figure. He had lost an eye—in a fight with the Orlovs, many people whispered. But he cut an imposing figure at court. He wore flowing silk robes and left his hair long. He was so ambitious that one diplomat predicted he might well end up governing Russia. Most importantly, he offered Catherine a swift mind to match her own.

Catherine installed Potemkin in the Winter Palace, and they quickly fell in love. They spent long hours together talking of life and politics. He sang to her. They amused each other with imitations of people

GREGORY POTEMKIN REPLACED Orlov as Catherine's closest adviser. Potemkin was famous for his ambition, brilliance, and wild mood swings.

at court. Observers noticed that Catherine's mood had improved tremendously. "I forget the whole world when I am with you," she wrote to Potemkin. "I have never been so happy as I am right now."

But with Pugachev's army threatening Moscow, Catherine could not afford to forget the world. Instead, she took control of the war effort with a new enthusiasm. She recruited loyal Cossacks and sent them chasing after Pugachev. She personally reviewed reports and maps from the field. In July 1774, she made peace with Abdülhamid I, the new Ottoman sultan, freeing more soldiers for the fight at home. By the end of the summer, her forces had pushed

Pugachev back to the Cossack territories, where his own people turned against him.

On September 15, 1774, the false Peter was tied up by his own aides and handed over to a local governor. Catherine's soldiers threw him into an iron cage and set off for Moscow. By the time his rolling prison reached the city, the rebel who had nearly seized the throne of Russia was begging to be put out of his misery. He was condemned to be quartered and then decapitated. But Catherine wanted to be seen as humane. She ordered Pugachev's head cut off first. He was executed on January 10, 1775.

THE IMPOSTER PUGACHEV (at right, with beard and ragged clothing) is brought to Moscow in chains. Pugachev had led a rebellion while claiming to be Peter III. Catherine had him executed.

CHAPTER 14

Love and Power

After two decades as empress, Catherine PREPARES FOR A GRAND CONQUEST.

CATHERINE APPROACHED THE AGE OF 50 hardened by the battles she had fought. When she first took power, she had high hopes for her reign. Armed with the powerful new ideas of the Enlightenment, how could she fail? An enlightened empress could bring justice, peace, and culture to the backward people of Russia.

Pugachev and his rebels shattered her optimism once and for all. Despite Catherine's good intentions, the people were still willing to take up arms against her. She felt compelled to answer them with force. In villages that supported Pugachev, the army set up gallows and torture wheels. They arrested people suspected of joining the rebellion and punished them mercilessly. The rebels had provoked Catherine into brutalities that could not have pleased her heroes, Voltaire and Diderot.

In her private life, Catherine still hungered for love and companionship. Rumor had it that she and Potemkin had married secretly near the end of 1774. But their relationship soon ran into trouble. They loved each other, but their habits clashed and they often argued. Potemkin was moody and disorganized. Catherine remained devoted to her work with discipline and steadiness. "We always fight about power," she wrote to him, "never about love."

Catherine and Potemkin soon reached an unusual agreement. He moved out of the Winter Palace, though he still held great power and advised her on all important issues. They saw each other often. But Catherine found companionship with a series of younger men.

Catherine's behavior shocked her fellow rulers in Europe. Many of them felt she should have married long before, or at least kept her personal affairs from becoming so public. King George III of Great Britain refused to offer knighthood to Potemkin when Catherine requested it. The Austrian empress, Maria Theresa, was so appalled she could only refer to Catherine as "that woman."

Despite their disapproval, observers in Europe had to admit one thing: Catherine had survived far longer than expected. She had ruled Russia for two decades, surviving countless plots against her life. She had expanded her empire west into Poland and south into the lands of the Ottoman Empire. And while she had failed to oust the Ottomans from Europe, her Russian soldiers made up one of the most feared fighting forces on earth.

Now, entering her third decade of rule, Catherine was about to surprise the world yet again. The peace with the Ottoman Empire in 1774 had given Russia important land along the Black Sea to the north and east of the Crimea. The Crimea itself—and its warm-water ports—had been declared independent from the Ottoman Empire.

In general, the treaty had been a resounding victory for Catherine. But she wanted more. If her troops could push even farther south and seize Constantinople, Russian merchant ships would have free access to the Mediterranean Sea. She would return Constantinople to the Christian world—and her grandchildren would reign over the largest empire on earth.

With help from Potemkin, Catherine set her plans in motion. Potemkin headed south to establish a presence in the new Russian territory around the Black Sea. He negotiated with the Tatars, Muslim tribesmen who lived along the border of the Ottoman Empire and had long been dominated by the Turks. Potemkin brought in thousands of German settlers to farm unused land. He built towns, churches, and modern shipyards. He constructed a fortress on the Dnieper River with barracks for 10,000 soldiers.

By 1783, the time had come to act. With Potemkin commanding thousands of troops along the Crimean

IN THIS BRITISH CARTOON, Catherine is portrayed as a bear (a symbol of Russia) under the control of Gregory Potemkin.

border, Catherine forced the khan, or leader, of the Crimea to step down. She renamed the area New Russia and sent Potemkin to take control. Once again, he imported colonists, founded towns, laid roads, and built universities, parks, vineyards, and shipyards.

Catherine had taken the first step toward a second war against the Turks. But before the fighting started, she decided to use her newest conquest for a grand display of Russian power. She wanted to show the world how far she had come since her days as a 15-year-old princess in a harsh, unfamiliar land.

CHAPTER 15

Grand Tour

Catherine travels to the Crimea
and makes sure THE WHOLE
WORLD IS WATCHING.

IN JANUARY 1787, THE 57-YEAR-OLD EMPRESS
left the snows of Russia for a grand tour of her lands
to the south. Her supply train included 1,000 horses,
164 sleds, and countless servants.

Potemkin had organized the trip, and he meant for
it to be a stunning display of Russian wealth and culture.
Many world leaders had been invited. They traveled in
14 luxury sleighs complete with cushions, carpets, sofas,
and tables. Servants hurried ahead to prepare each

stop with new dishes, linens, the finest food, and other luxuries. Everywhere along the way, Catherine was hailed as a conquering empress.

The sleighs took the party as far as the city of Kiev, where they boarded boats to journey down the Dnieper River. Each boat had a music room, a salon, a library, and cabins supplied with fresh water. Acting on Potemkin's orders, a labor force had cleared the Dnieper by blowing up rocks and leveling sandbars.

Potemkin managed the journey carefully in order to present Russia in the best light possible. One ambassador charged that Potemkin had erected fake house fronts on the riverbank and decorated them with garlands, carpets, and smiling Russians. Most likely, he did not go that far, but his efforts to paint his achievements in the best possible light became known as "Potemkin villages."

After the river voyage, Catherine met with her former lover, Stanislas Poniatowski, now king of Poland, and Joseph II, who had ruled the Austrian Empire since his mother's death in 1780. They spent several nights sleeping in open camps on the rugged steppes. "What a strange journey," Joseph said, "with Catherine II and the ministers of France and England, wandering in the desert of the Tatars. It is a completely new page of history!"

Catherine was proud to be the author of this new page. She showed no fear when the group reached the Crimean border and entered the conquered country. She hardly flinched as 1,200 fierce Tatar warriors approached on horseback. She insisted that her new

RAGGED PEASANTS WERE HIDDEN away (at left) as Catherine and other rulers paraded through the Crimea. Critics claimed Potemkin built entire fake villages to impress the visitors.

subjects were loyal—and she was right. The Tatars had come to escort her to the former khan's palace in the city of Bakhchisarai. One Tatar horseman even dashed ahead to stop her carriage when its horses bolted down a steep hill.

The encounter with the Tatars proved Catherine's genius as a conqueror. Rather than force Russian ways on the local population, she had protected their religion, customs, and language. For now, the Tatars had little to protest.

Catherine found the Crimea beautiful. The olive and palm trees, warm southern skies, and overflowing gardens seemed like paradise. The trip ended with a banquet at the Black Sea port of Sevastopol. Through the palace windows, Catherine's party had a view of Potemkin's warships. He had built the entire fleet in less than two years, a testament to the power of the Russian military. The message was clear. The fleet was just two days from Constantinople. He needed only Catherine's signal to attack.

CHAPTER 16

War and Revolution

CATHERINE BATTLES THE OTTOMANS abroad and radicals at home.

CATHERINE'S GRAND VOYAGE THROUGH the Crimea proved to be the high point of her reign. Within months, the Turks had responded to her show of force in the Crimea. They arrested the Russian minister in Constantinople and declared war on Russia. In August 1787, Catherine ordered an attack against the Ottoman Empire. Now was the time for Potemkin's supposedly invincible Black Sea fleet to show its worth.

Unfortunately, the fleet had been built for public relations rather than for war. To finish it in time for Catherine's journey, Potemkin had used wood that had not been properly prepared to resist water. The ships were destroyed in a storm before they could meet the Turks in battle.

The loss of his fleet plunged Potemkin into a moody fit. He wrote Catherine that he wanted to retreat. He begged her to negotiate peace with the Turks before it was too late. He would step down and confine himself to a monastery, he said.

Alarmed, Catherine wrote back. "Fortify your mind and soul!" she urged him. This was no time for retreat.

Catherine was also faced with new troubles in the north. In 1788, the Swedes declared war on Russia. Their navy menaced Russia's Baltic coast. Wearily, Catherine received news about battle after battle as the two wars raged on.

However, no battle report alarmed the empress as much as the news from France. In 1789, revolutionaries unseated King Louis XVI and were talking of forming a republic free of any king. Laborers had taken over the streets. Radicals controlled the government. And Louis was being held as a prisoner in his own country.

The French Revolution horrified Catherine. She knew it had been fueled in part by the Enlightenment ideas she had once embraced. But it was one thing to speak up for

POTEMKIN LEADS AN ATTACK on a castle in Ukraine, a land to the southeast of Russia.

the rights of man, quite another to rise up against the government! France, she said, had "gone to ruin."

Catherine grew terrified that the "French infection" would spread to Russia. She mobilized the Secret Branch to track down revolutionaries in St. Petersburg and Moscow. She banned her old friend Voltaire's books in Russia. She even outlawed the sale of the red caps worn by French revolutionaries.

In the summer of 1790, a writer named Alexander Radishchev published a book that called for liberating the serfs. It was a proposal that Catherine herself had once made, but now she saw Radishchev's book as a challenge to her authority. She seized all the copies and had the author arrested and exiled to Siberia.

By the following year, Catherine was eager to end the war with the Turks. She sent Potemkin to meet with Turkish ambassadors, but Potemkin left the conference without success. He had fallen ill. He scribbled a note to Catherine before he boarded a carriage with a doctor. "Little Mother, gracious sovereign," the note read. "I can no longer endure my torments."

The carriage didn't get far. The rutted road jolted Potemkin until he begged to stop. The doctor helped him out, and he lay on the grass. An hour later, the mighty man died by the side of the road. The doctor closed Potemkin's one eye. He laid a coin over the eyelid, as was the custom.

A messenger brought Catherine the news in St. Petersburg. She fainted. Her doctors put her to bed sobbing. She shut herself in her room and refused to see anyone.

When the empress emerged, she imposed a strict period of mourning on her court. Potemkin's death would cast a shadow on the rest of Catherine's life. In January 1792, she finally signed a peace treaty with the Turks, but it was not the triumph she had sought. She had added the Crimea to her growing empire, but she would never gain possession of Constantinople.

CHAPTER 17

A Good Heart

After 34 years, Catherine reaches
THE END OF HER REIGN.

AT 65, CATHERINE HAD GROWN STOUT but lost little energy. She wore simple gray gowns and no jewelry so she could dress quickly and get to work. Her greyhounds and her grandchildren were her greatest pleasures. Her teeth were gone now. She moved slowly. Her hair was white. Foreign newspapers were fond of announcing her death. Yet here she was, alive and still the empress of Russia.

She had seven grandchildren in all. She loved to walk with them through the palace gardens. She

CATHERINE HAD PROVED to be one of the shrewdest and most powerful rulers in the world.

didn't care for her son Paul, but she felt that his son Alexander would make a fine emperor.

Her last days were spent as always, governing her people with a firm hand. She still loved to read and write, though she needed glasses and a magnifying glass to see the words. She laughed at the judgmental accounts of her romantic affairs still circulating in the Western press. She hoped to be remembered as a humane and enlightened monarch. Still, her youthful optimism had long since faded. The revolutionary ideas of the Enlightenment had cost Louis XVI his head and plunged all of Western Europe into war. She did not feel she had accomplished what she set out to do and didn't like to hear her subjects call her Catherine the Great.

From the day she began planning to seize the throne of Russia, Catherine had created her own destiny. Now, she longed to shape the way the world remembered her. Catherine wrote her own epitaph in a letter to a friend:

Here lies Catherine the Second, born in Stettin on April 21, 1729. She came to Russia in 1744 to marry Peter III. At the age of 14, she formed the threefold project of pleasing her husband, Empress Elizabeth, and the nation. She neglected nothing to succeed in this. Eighteen years of boredom and solitude made her read plenty of books. Arrived on the throne of Russia, she desired its good and sought to procure for her subjects happiness, liberty, and propriety. She forgave easily and hated no one; indulgent, easy to live with, naturally cheerful, with a republican soul and a good heart, she had friends, she found work easy, she liked good society and the arts.

Catherine had a stroke on November 16, 1796, and died the following morning. After her death, her son Paul reopened his father's tomb and placed Catherine's body beside the husband she had detested.

Wicked?

After her death, the empress of Russia was quickly given the name she had rejected during her life: Catherine the Great. All across the world, people agreed that her life had been remarkable. She had survived far longer and accomplished more than anyone had thought possible.

So why did she develop a reputation for wickedness? First of all, the more conservative visitors from Western Europe were scandalized by her romantic life. Women—even powerful women—were supposed to marry and stay married. But Catherine chose to fall in love again and again.

The second charge against Catherine haunted her entire reign. Though she never dared to admit it, she most likely ordered Alexis Orlov to murder her husband, Tsar Peter.

Catherine had grand plans for her country when

she took the throne at 33. She had spent years reading Voltaire, Rousseau, and Diderot, absorbing the new ideas of the time. As empress, she had a chance to put those ideas into practice. She could make books and education available to an illiterate people. She could promote freedom of thought. She could devise a system of laws that would apply equally to all people. She could even work toward freeing the millions of Russians who lived in near slavery as serfs.

In the end, Catherine's accomplishments fell short of her goals. Her attempts at reform were often blocked by nobles who did not want to give up power. She responded to Pugachev's rebellion with a brutal, bloody crackdown. And once the French Revolution erupted, Catherine gave up her own ideals in order to silence Radischev and others whom she saw as a threat.

But, as Catherine noted when Diderot was visiting, she lived in the real world. And in the real world, people are generally frightened by change. Despite her people's mistrust, Catherine had some remarkable accomplishments. She built dozens of towns, took a census, and mapped the provinces. She organized and reformed government in St. Petersburg. She built orphanages and made prisons more humane. She established schools for both boys and girls. She promoted books and reading and founded a medical college. And she expanded the Russian Empire until it stretched from the Baltic to eastern Siberia.

Sixty-five years after Catherine's death, the serfs of Russia finally won their freedom. Tsar Alexander II signed the order in 1861. He was the great-grandson of Catherine the Great.

WHEN CATHERINE the Great died, she was buried next to the person she probably hated most in the world— her late husband, Tsar Peter.

Timeline of Terror

1729

1729: Catherine (Princess Sophie) is born.

1744: Princess Sophie and her mother go to Russia to meet Empress Elizabeth and her son, Peter.

1745: Sophie marries Peter and changes her name to Catherine.

1754: Catherine gives birth to a son, Paul.

1756: The Seven Years' War begins; Catherine exchanges letters with Elizabeth's chancellor.

1757: Catherine gives birth to a daughter, Anna.

1758: Elizabeth accuses Catherine of treason for meddling in the war; Catherine clears herself.

1761: Empress Elizabeth dies; Peter becomes tsar.

1762: Catherine gives birth to a son, Alexis.

1762: With help from Gregory Orlov, captain of palace guard, Catherine seizes power from Peter, who is later killed.

1767: Empress Catherine publishes the *Great Instruction*, calling for equal rights under the law.

1768: Catherine goes to war against the Ottoman Empire, hoping to seize the Crimea.

1773: Catherine breaks ties with longtime companion Gregory Orlov.

1774: Catherine brings Gregory Potemkin to court as a companion and adviser.

1774: Catherine ruthlessly puts down a peasant rebellion led by Emilian Pugachev.

1783: Catherine annexes the Crimea.

1787: Potemkin organizes a grand tour of the Crimea for Catherine; the second war with Ottoman Empire begins.

1790: French Revolution prompts Catherine to crack down on free speech in Russia.

1796: Catherine dies.

1796

GLOSSARY

alliance (uh-LYE-uhnss) *noun* an agreement to work together

archenemy (arch-EN-uh-mee) *noun* a person's worst enemy

baptism (BAP-tiz-im) *noun* a ritual in which water is sprinkled on someone's head or someone is immersed in water as a symbol of acceptance into Christianity

barracks (BA-ruhks) *noun* buildings to house on-duty soldiers

bureaucrat (BYUR-oh-crat) *noun* an official in a governmental department

Cossacks (KOH-saks) *noun* people of southern Russia, Ukraine, and Siberia who were known for their independence and military skill

coup (KOO) *noun* a sudden, violent, and illegal seizure of power

courtier (KOR-tee-uhr) *noun* a person who attends a royal court as a companion or adviser to the king or queen

desolate (DESS-uh-luhht) *adjective* empty of warmth or comfort

devout (di-VOUT) *adjective* devoted to living by the rules of a religion

elite (i-LEET) *noun* a group of people who have special privileges or abilities

empire (EM-pire) *noun* a group of countries or regions that have the same ruler

Enlightenment (en-LITE-uhn-muhnt) *noun* a philosophical movement of the 18th century that emphasized the use of human reason to build a better world

epitaph (EP-ih-taff) *noun* a short description of someone who has died

exiled (EG-zild) *adjective* sent away from one's homeland

humane (hyoo-MAYN) *adjective* sympathetic and merciful

illiterate (i-LIT-ur-it) *adjective* not able to read or write

infirmities (in-FIRM-ih-teez) *noun* physical or mental weaknesses khan (KON) *noun* a ruler of Turkish or Tatar tribes during the time of Catherine the Great

monastery (MON-uh-ster-ee) *noun* a group of buildings where monks live and work

mosque (MOSK) *noun* a building used by Muslims for worship

nobility (noh-BIL-ih-tee) *noun* the people in a country or state who have been born into wealthy families and have the highest social rank

open letter (OH-puhn LET-ur) *noun* a letter that is addressed to a person but meant to be read by a wide audience

pawn (PAWN) *noun* a person used by others for their own purposes

Protestant (PROT-uh-stuhnt) *noun* a Christian who does not belong to the Roman Catholic or Orthodox Church

pustule (PUSS-tyul) *noun* a small blister or pimple on the skin containing pus

Russian Orthodox (RUHSH-in OR-thuh-doks) *adjective* describing the major church of Christianity in Russia

scythe (SITH) *noun* a tool with a large, curved blade used for cutting crops

serf (SURF) *noun* in Russia, a peasant laborer forced to work on the estate of a noble landowner

sovereign (SOV-ruhn) *noun* the supreme leader of a country

steppe (STEP) *noun* a vast, treeless plain

sultan (SUHLT-uhn) *noun* an emperor or ruler of a Muslim monarchy

treason (TREE-zuhn) *noun* the crime of betraying one's country

tsar (ZAR) *noun* the emperor, or "Caesar," of Russia

tyrannical (tye-RAN-ih-kuhl) *adjective* ruling others in a cruel or unjust way

valet (val-AY) *noun* a personal attendant

FIND OUT MORE

Here are some books and websites with more information about Catherine the Great and her times.

BOOKS

Hatt, Christine. **Catherine the Great (Judge for Yourself)**. Milwaukee: World Almanac Library, 2004. (64 pages) *A thought-provoking book that asks readers to draw their own conclusions about the legacy of Catherine the Great.*

King, David. **The Enlightenment (People at the Center of)**. Farmington Hills, MI: Blackbirch Press, 2005. (48 pages) *Profiles the key players of the Enlightenment movement, including Catherine the Great.*

Rogers, Stillman D. **Russia (Enchantment of the World, Second Series)**. New York: Children's Press, 2002. (144 pages) *Describes the history, geography, culture, and people of Russia.*

Strickler, James E. **Russia of the Tsars**. San Diego: Lucent Books, 1998. (96 pages) *This book covers the history of Russia under the tsars, from the 1500s to 1917.*

Whitelaw, Nancy. **Catherine the Great and the Enlightenment of Russia**. Greensboro, NC: Morgan Reynolds, 2005. (160 pages) *A highly readable book about the extraordinarily dramatic life of Catherine the Great.*

WEBSITES

http://www.bartleby.com/67/russia04.html
A chart from the Encyclopedia of World History showing the Russian tsars from 1645–1917.

http://www.bbc.co.uk/history/historic_figures/catherine_the_great.shtml
BBC History's profile of Catherine the Great.

http://www.hermitagemuseum.org/html_En/index.html
The official website of the State Hermitage Museum in St. Petersburg, Russia—a world-renowned art museum established by Catherine the Great.

http://www.pbs.org/weta/faceofrussia/intro.html
This companion website to the PBS series The Face of Russia *offers an excellent timeline and other resources on Russian history.*

For Grolier subscribers:
http://go.grolier.com searches: Catherine II; Elizabeth, Empress of Russia; Peter III (Russia); Orlov (family); Potemkin, Grigori

Author's Note and Bibliography

How did a young girl who came to a foreign country at 15, with little knowledge of its culture, religion, or language, end up ruling the Russian Empire?

Catherine was smart. She had both style and substance. And she learned early to create an image of herself that was larger than life. But before this, she nearly lost everything because of one ill-chosen dress.

When Catherine first arrived in Russia as Princess Sophie, she was wearing a pink dress. Little did she know that pink was the empress's favorite color and that she reserved it for her own use. Elizabeth had forbidden the ladies at court to wear it. In fact, it's said that one woman's tongue was cut out for daring to wear pink.

Fortunately for Catherine, the empress did not hold her misstep against her. And after this brush with fate, Catherine worked hard to micro-manage her public life—right down to the clothes she wore.

The following books have proved most helpful in researching this book:

Cruise, Mark & Hilde Hoogenboom. The Memoirs of Catherine the Great. New York: Modern Library, 2005.

Erickson, Carolly. Great Catherine. New York: Crown Publishers, Inc., 1994.

Rounding, Virginia. Catherine the Great, Love, Sex, and Power. New York: St. Martin's Press, 2006.

Thomson, Scott. Catherine and the Expansion. London: English University Press, 1955.

Troyat, Henri (Pinkham, Joan, translator). Catherine the Great. New York: Penguin Group (USA) Inc., 1994.

I'm grateful to my keen-eyed editor, Tod Olson, and to my fabulous fellow researcher, Aubrie Koenig, for their insights into the young princess who became Catherine the Great.

—Zu Vincent